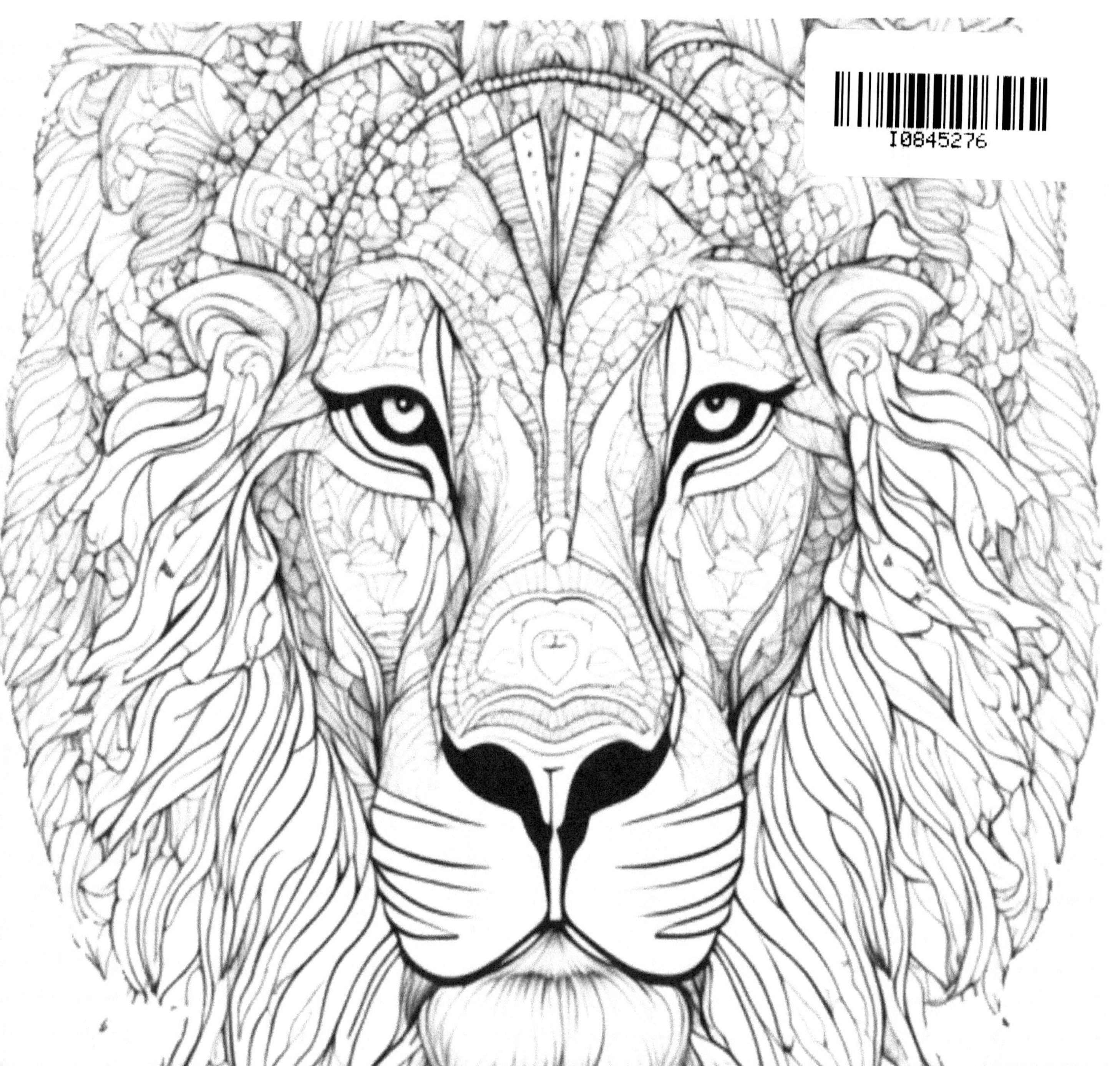

Blank Canvas

START YOUR MASTERPIECE

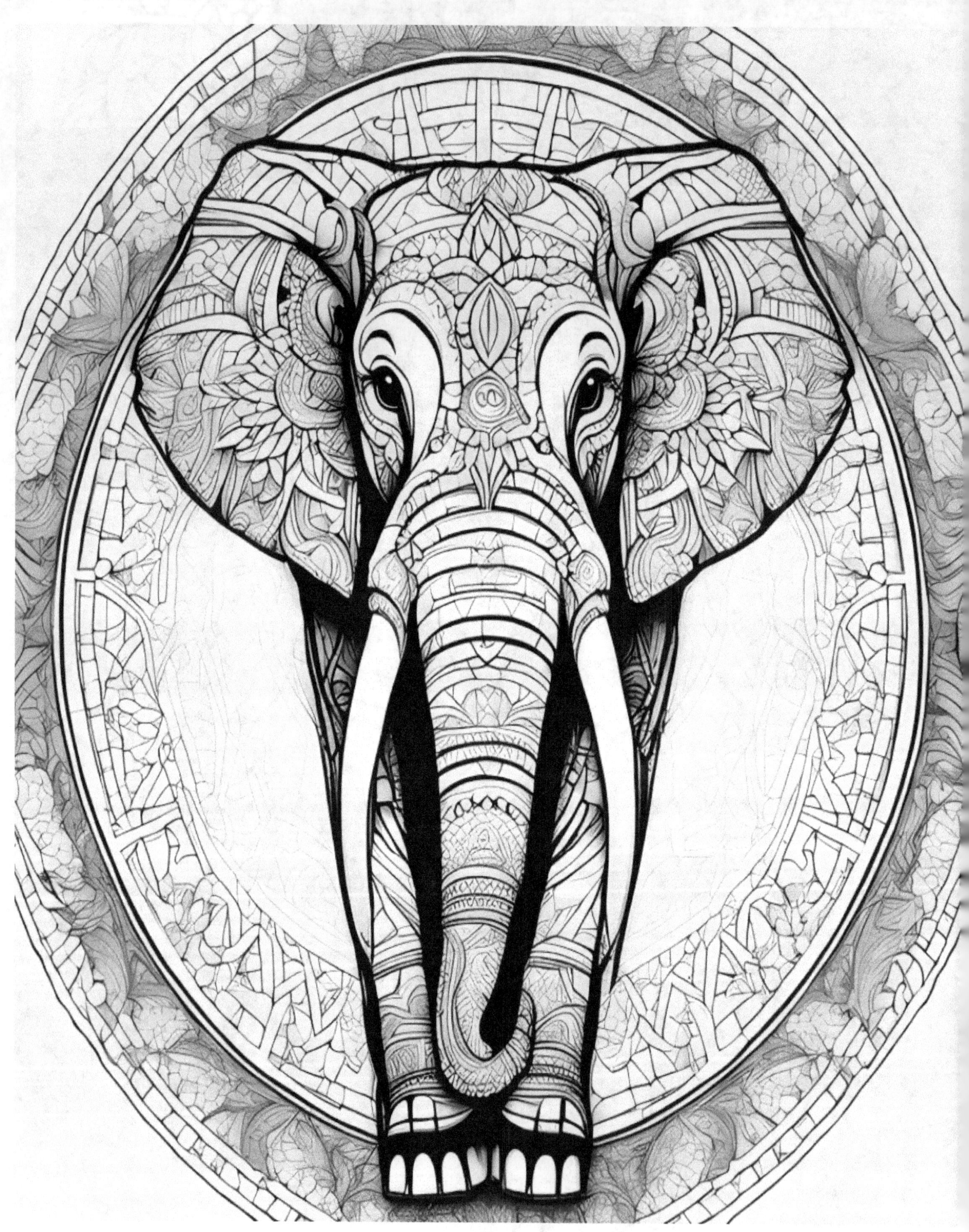

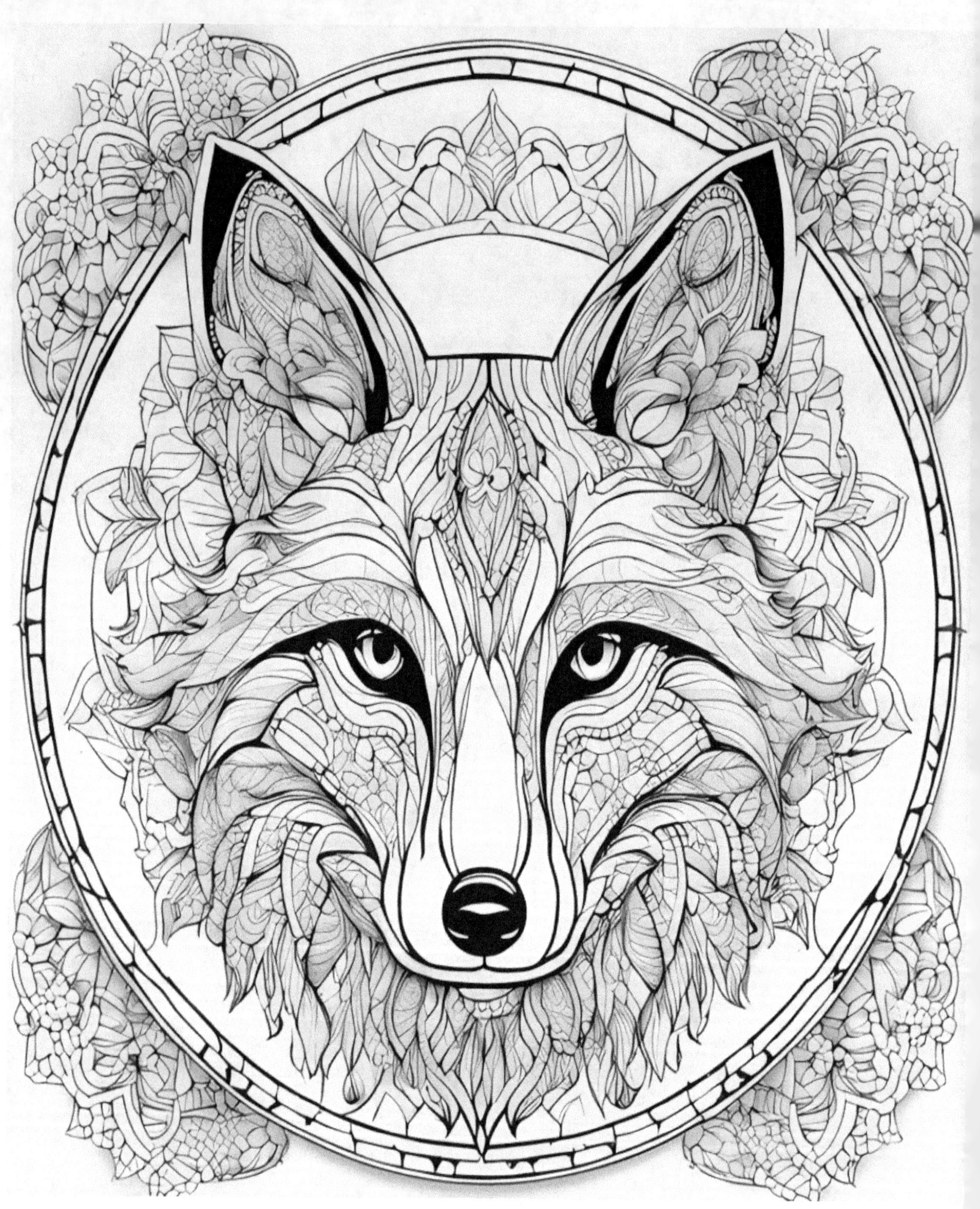

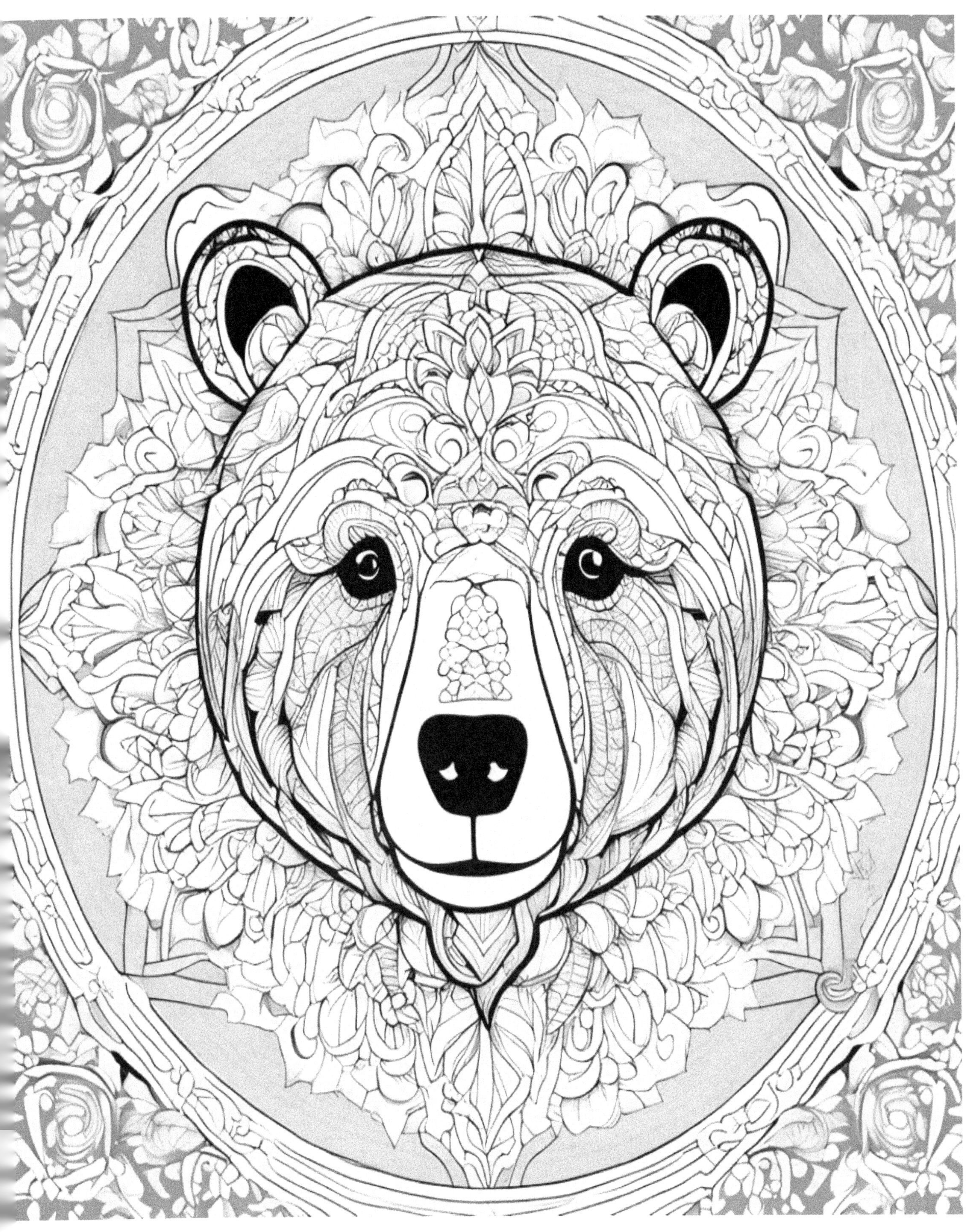

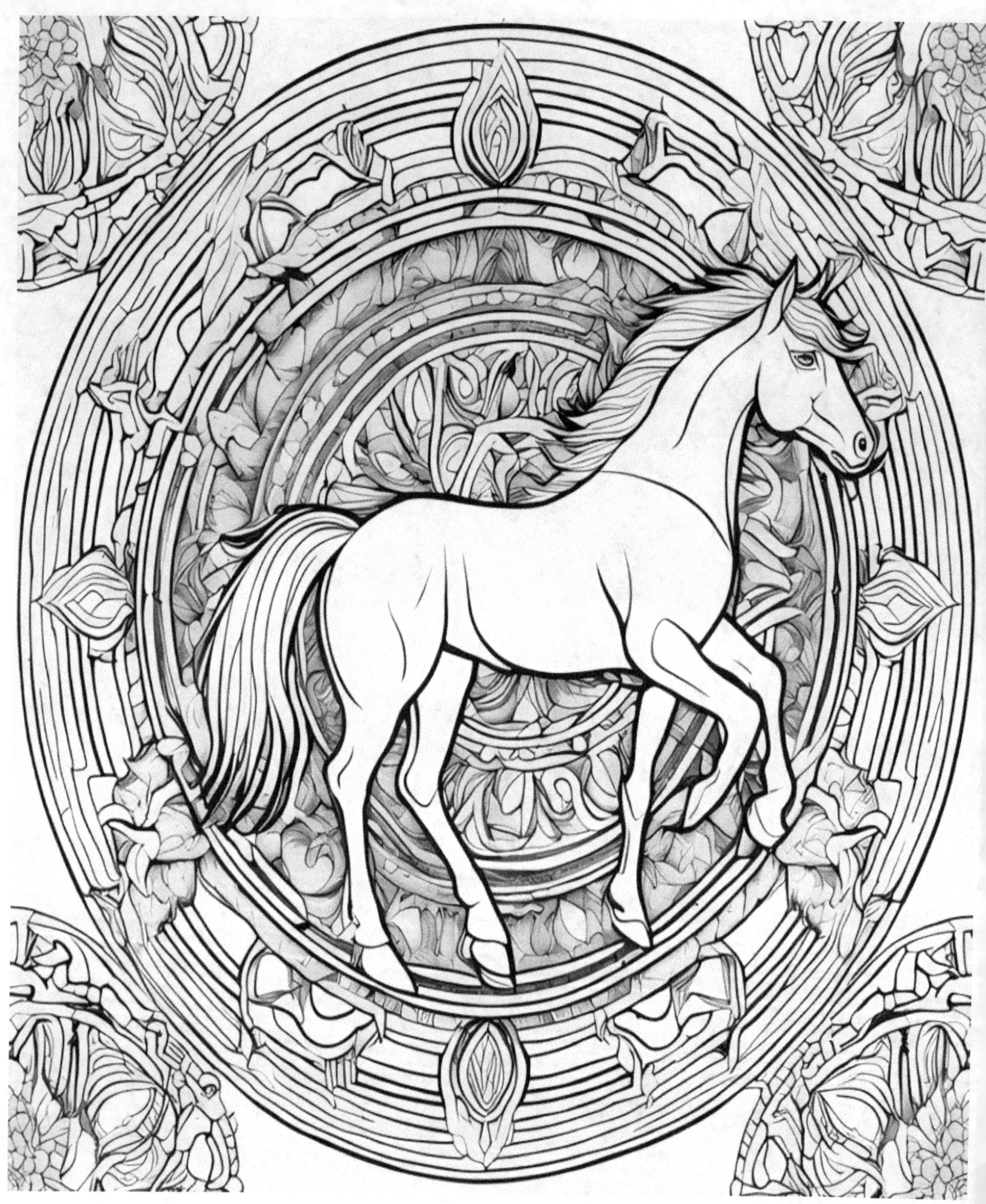

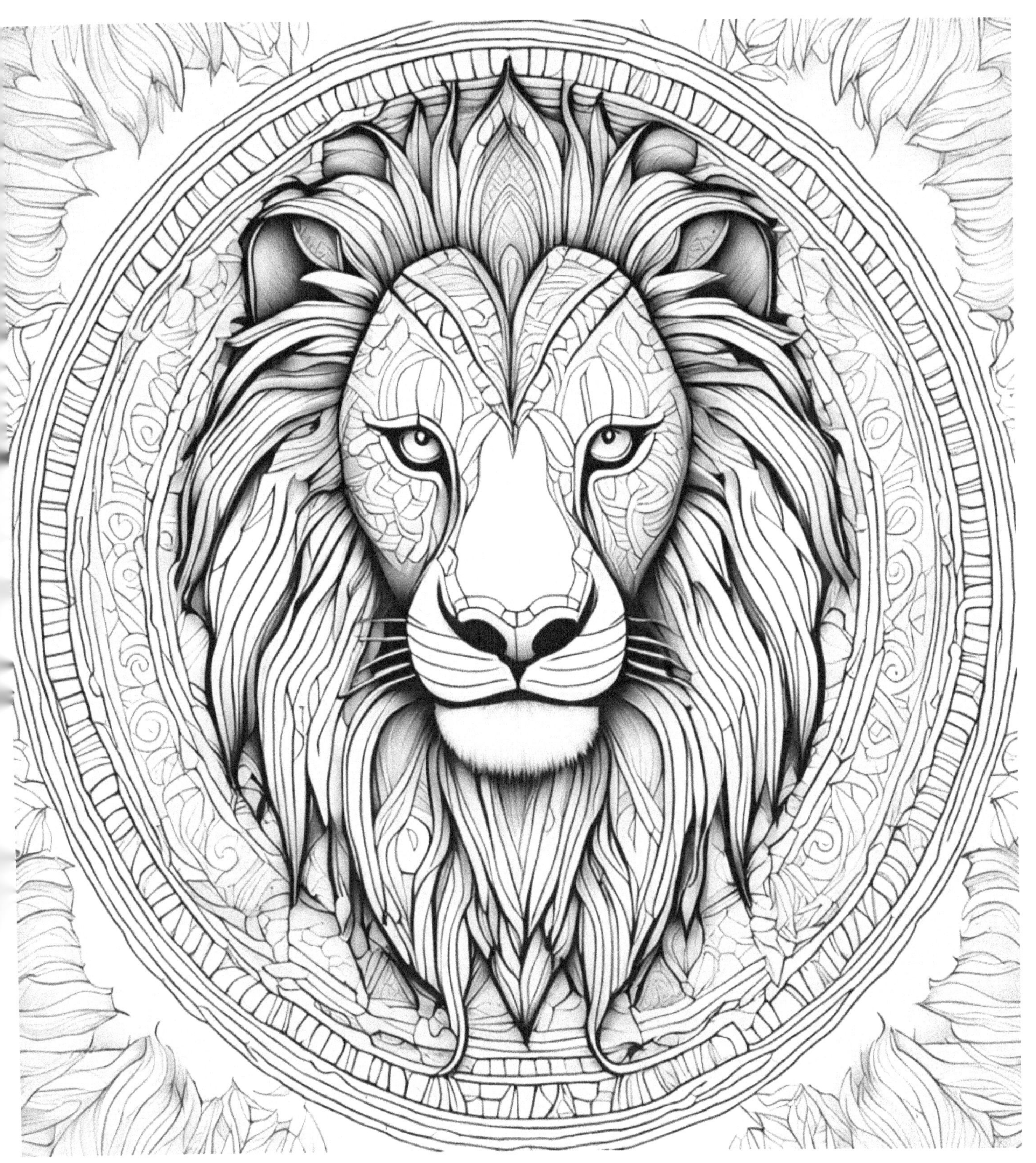

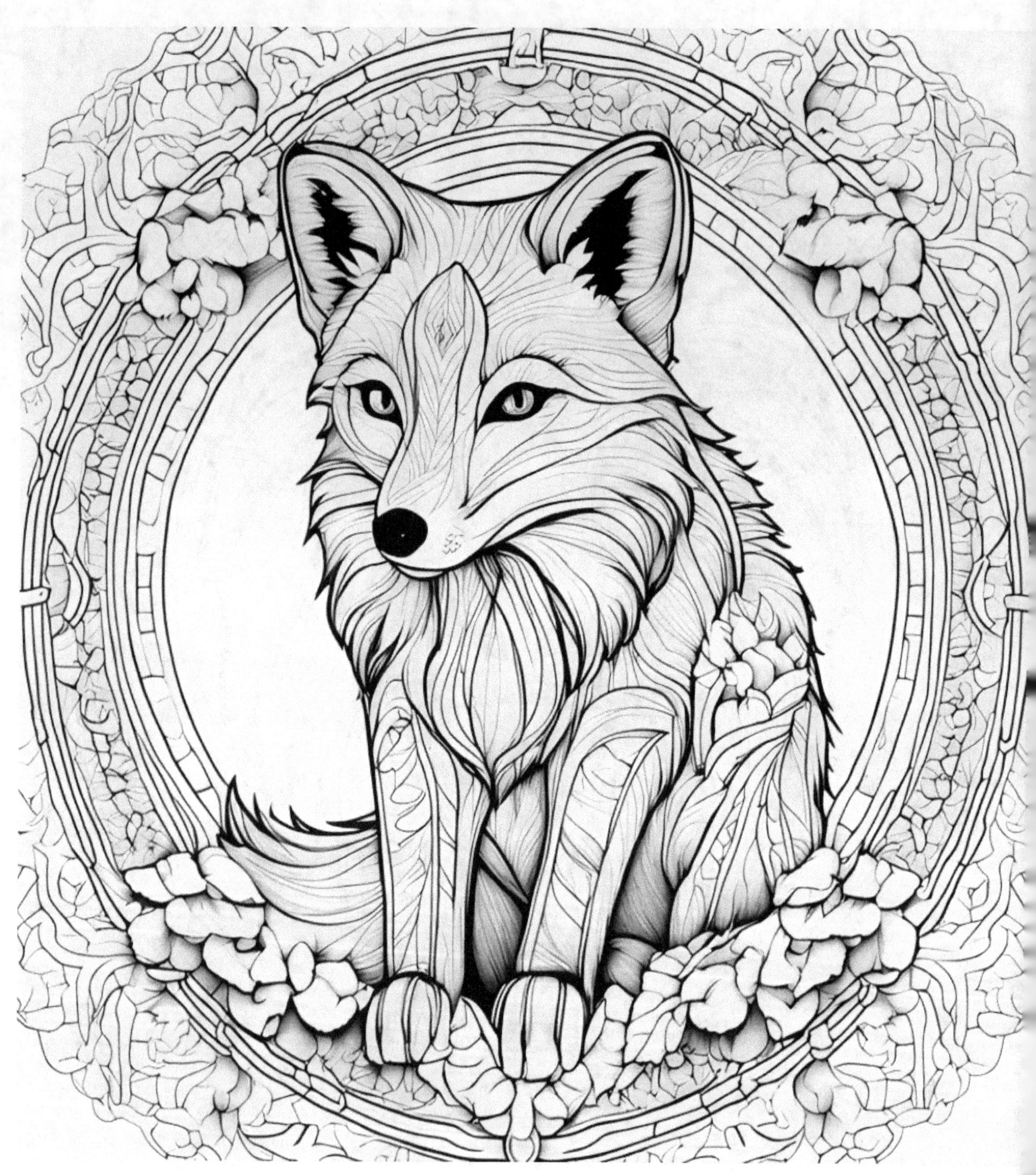

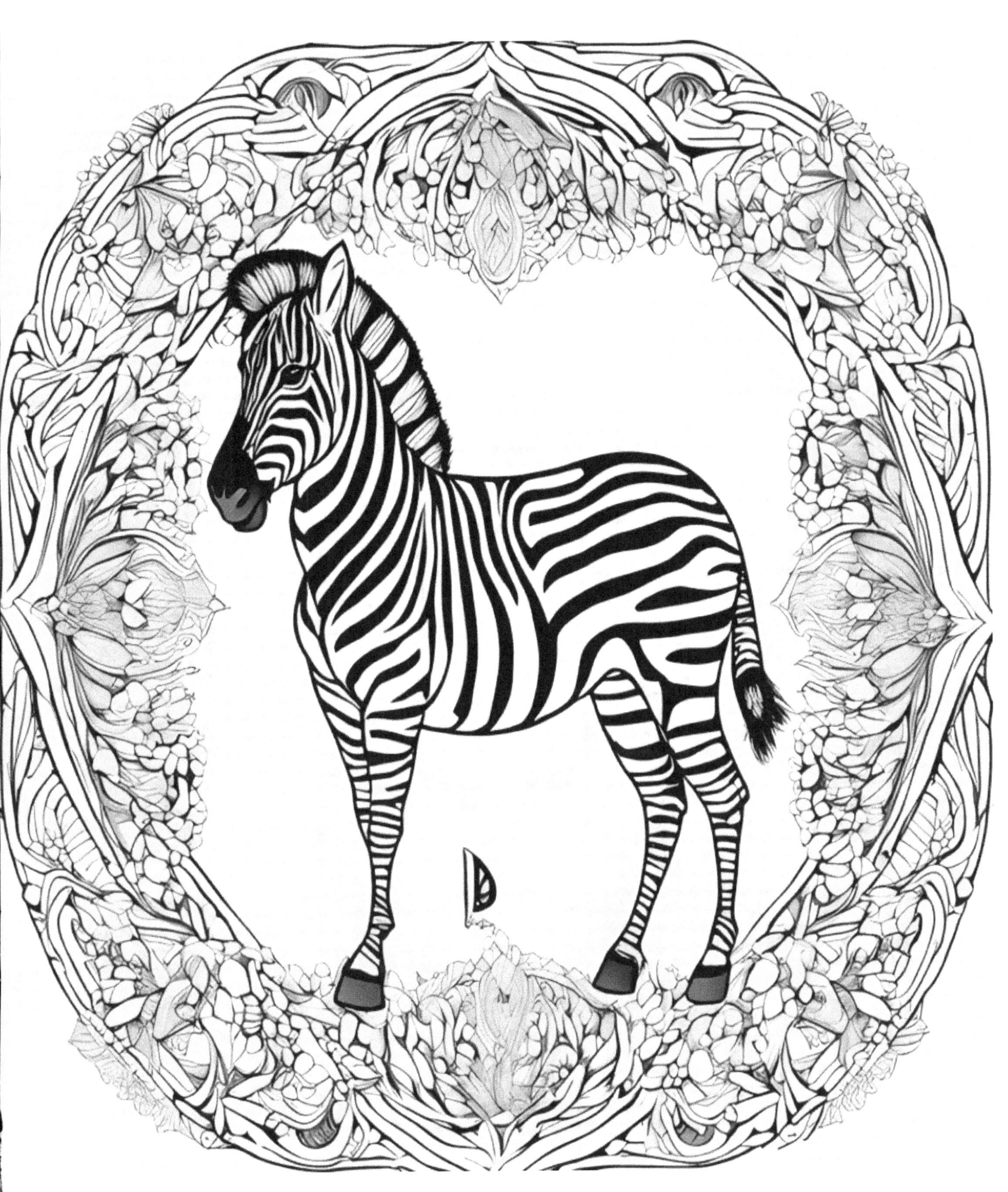

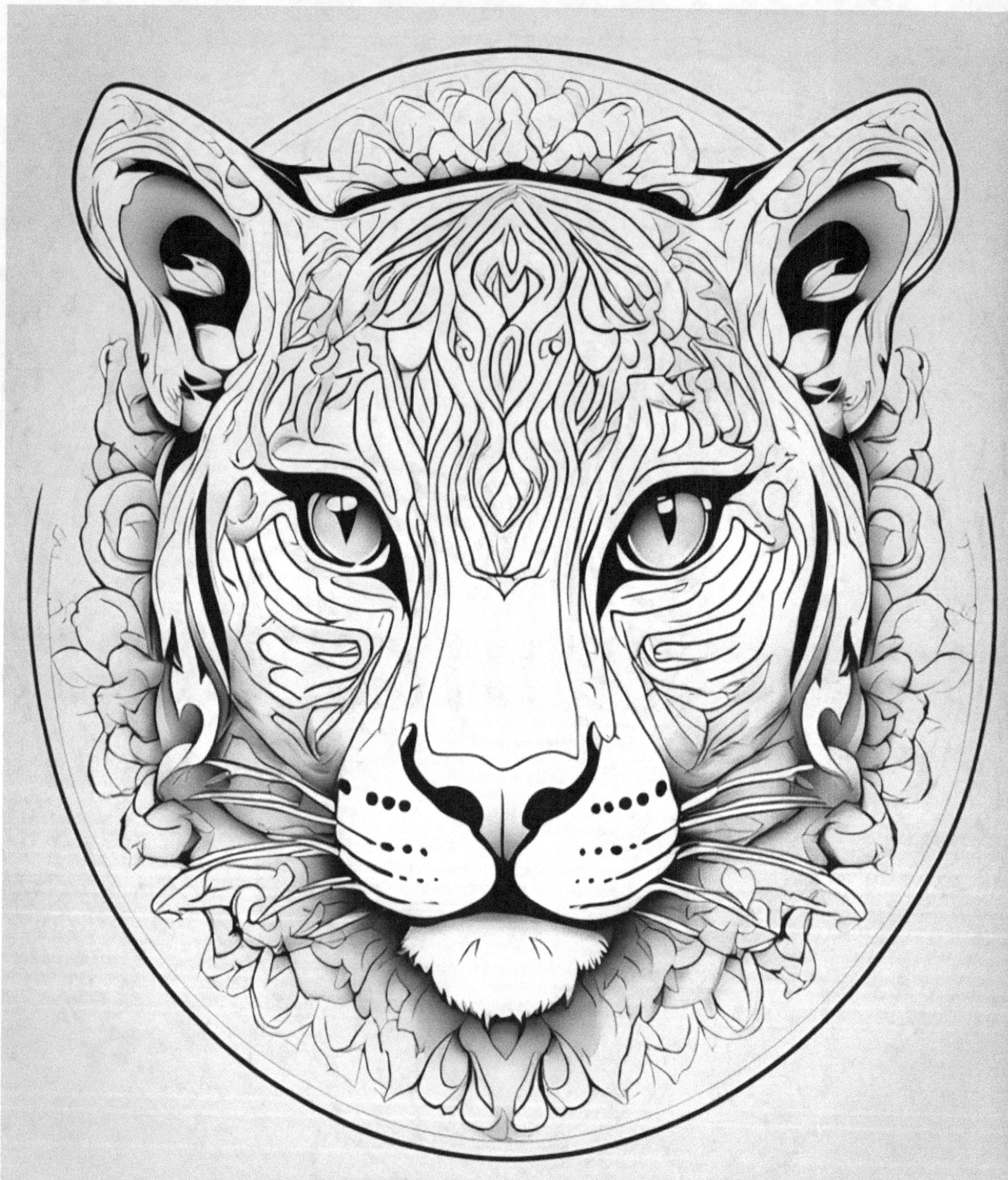

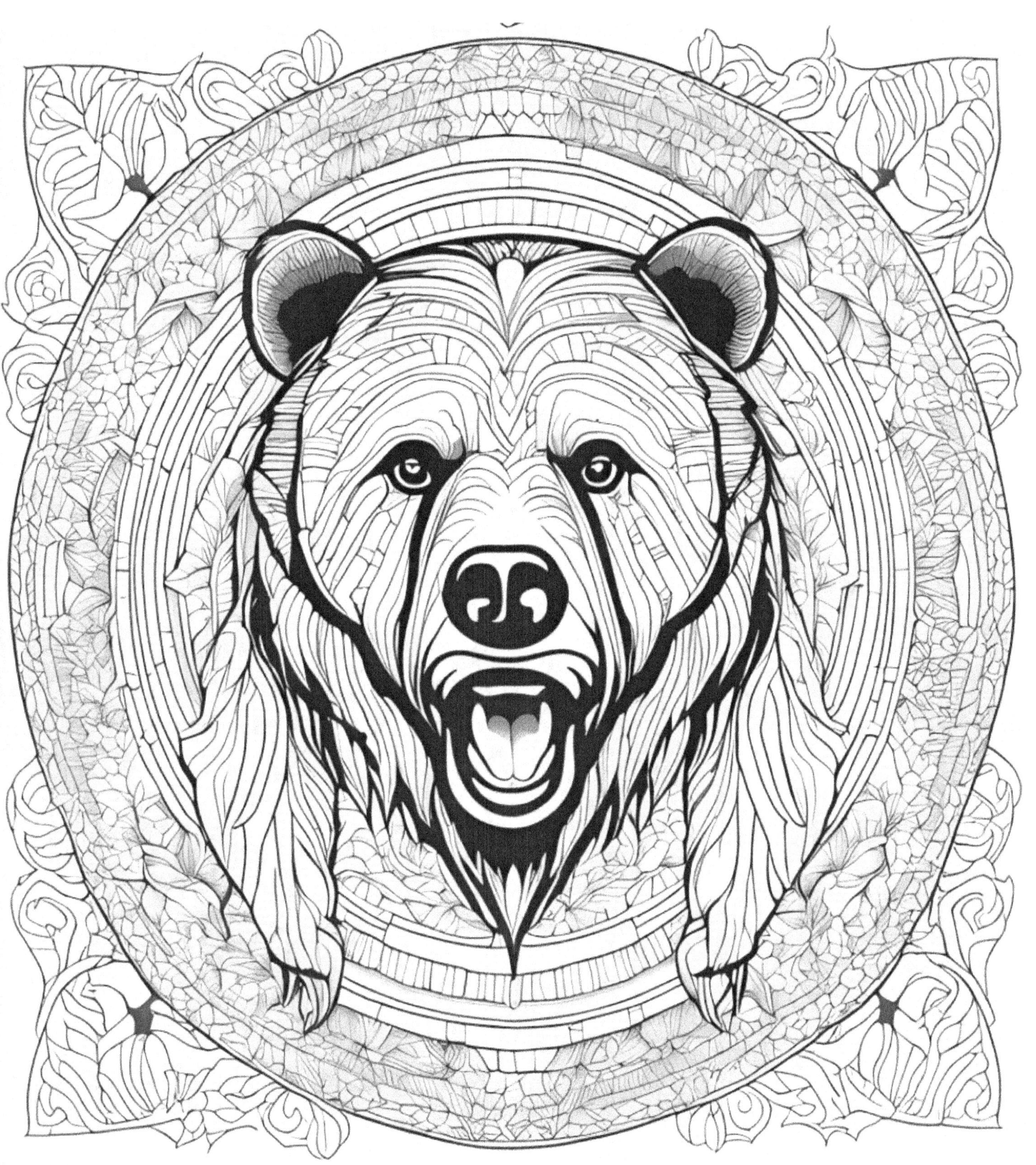

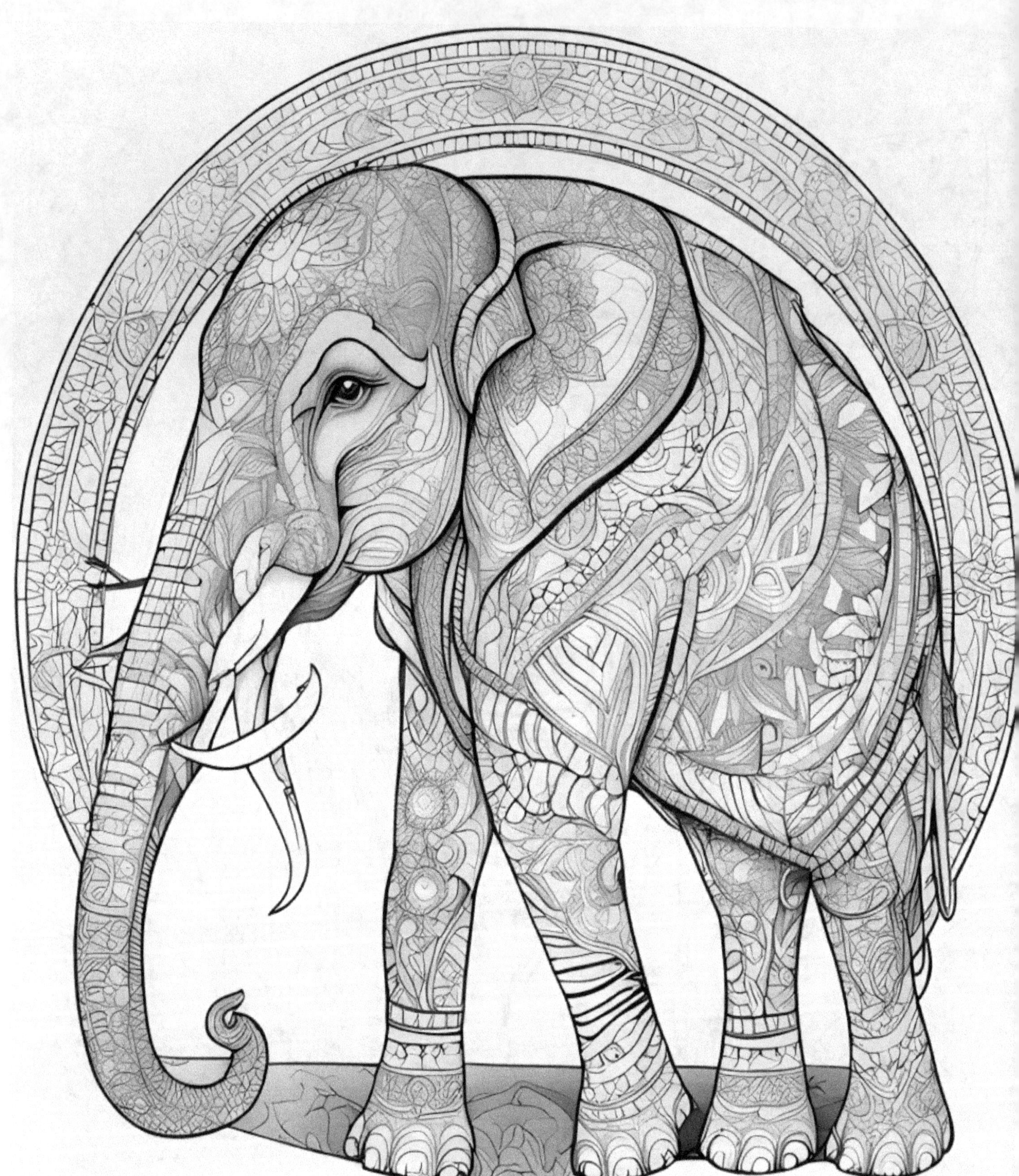

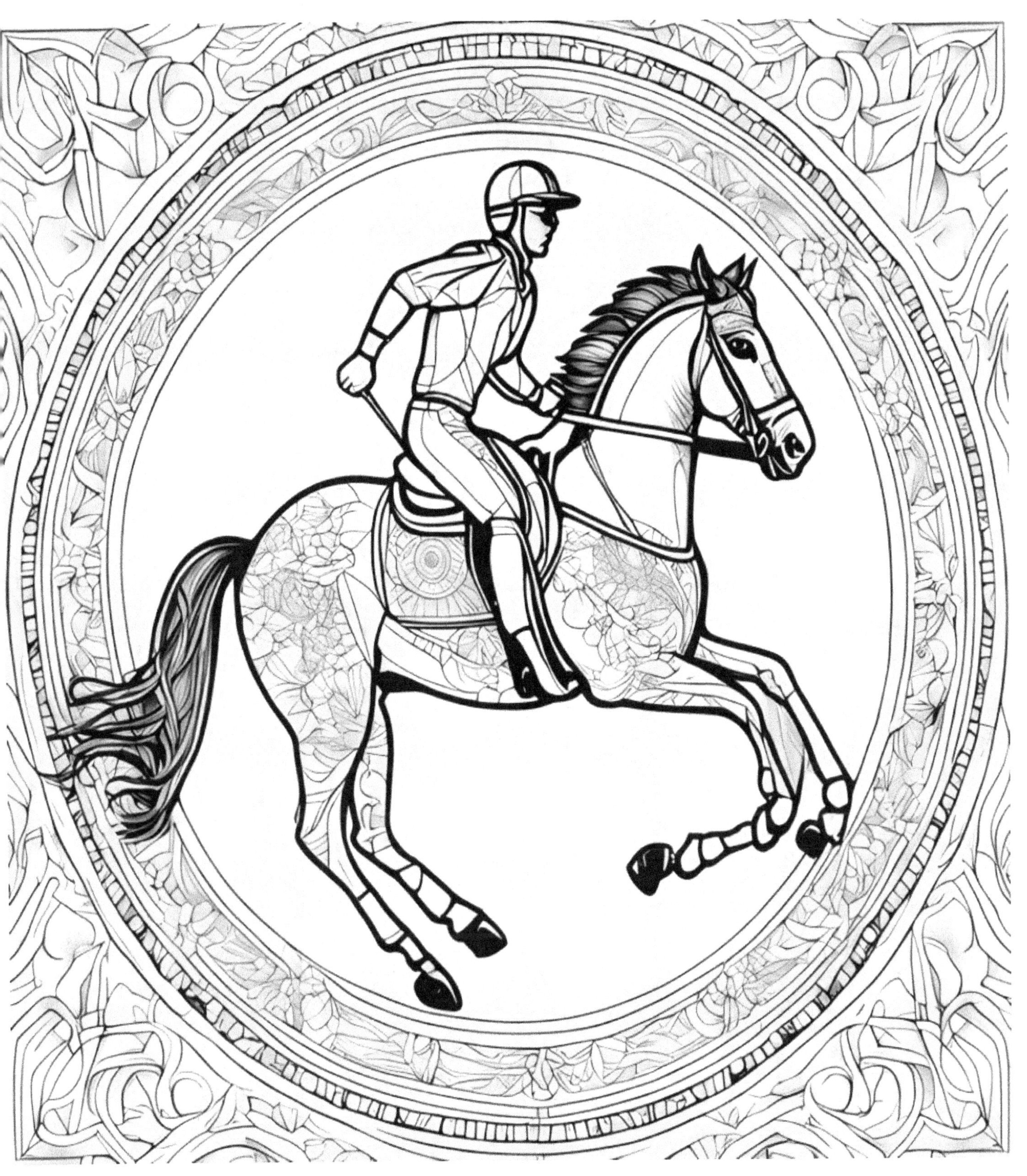

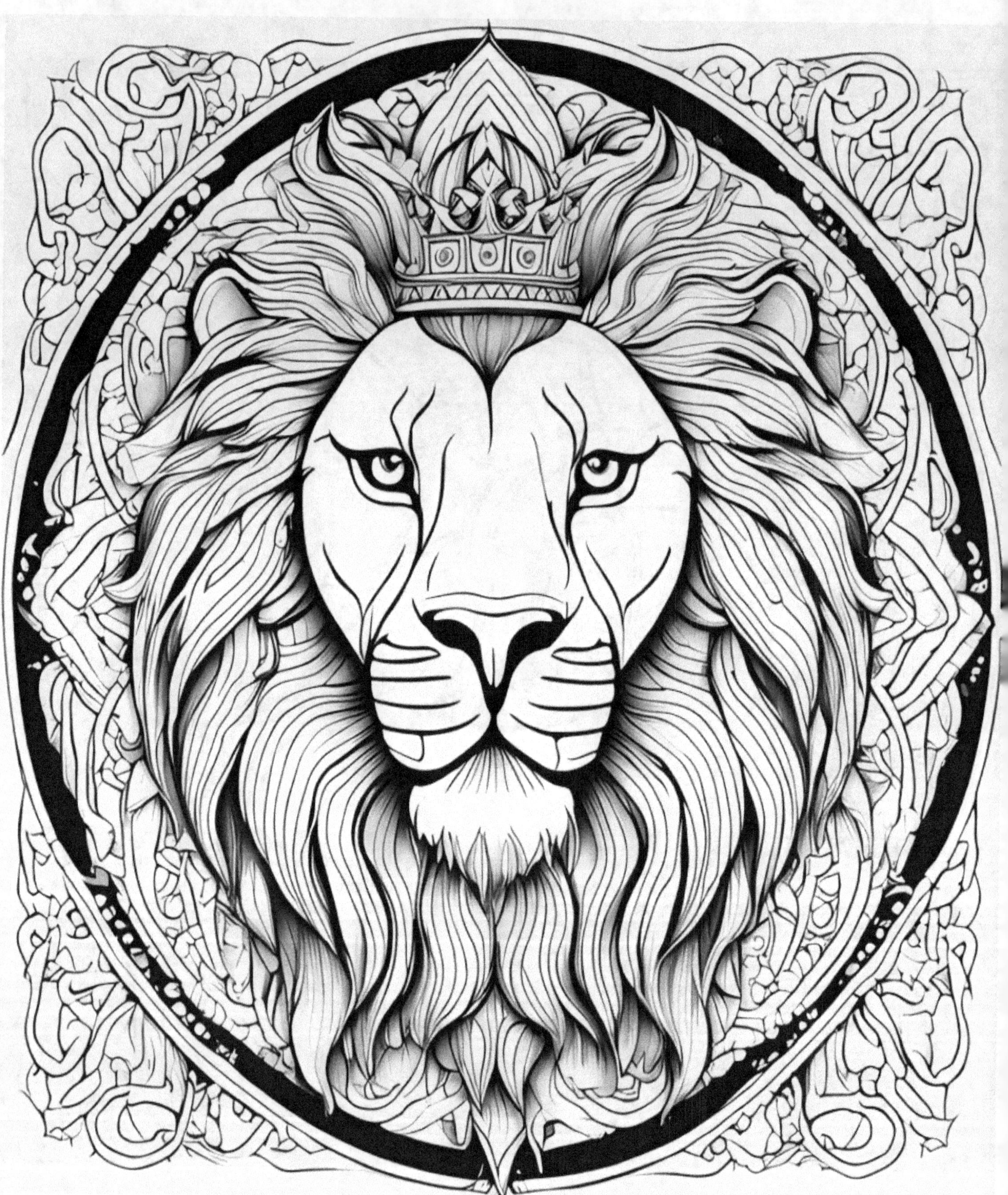

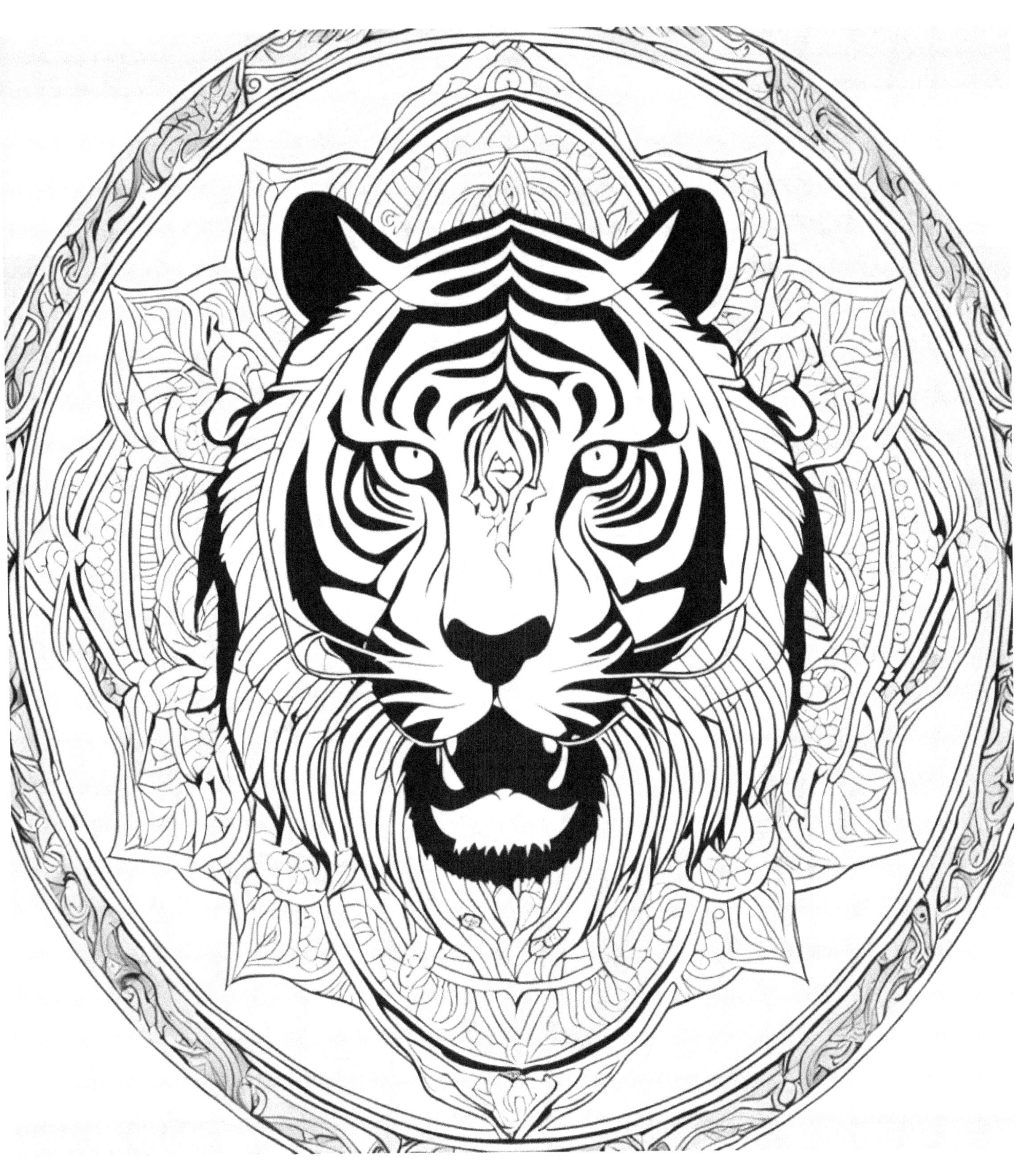

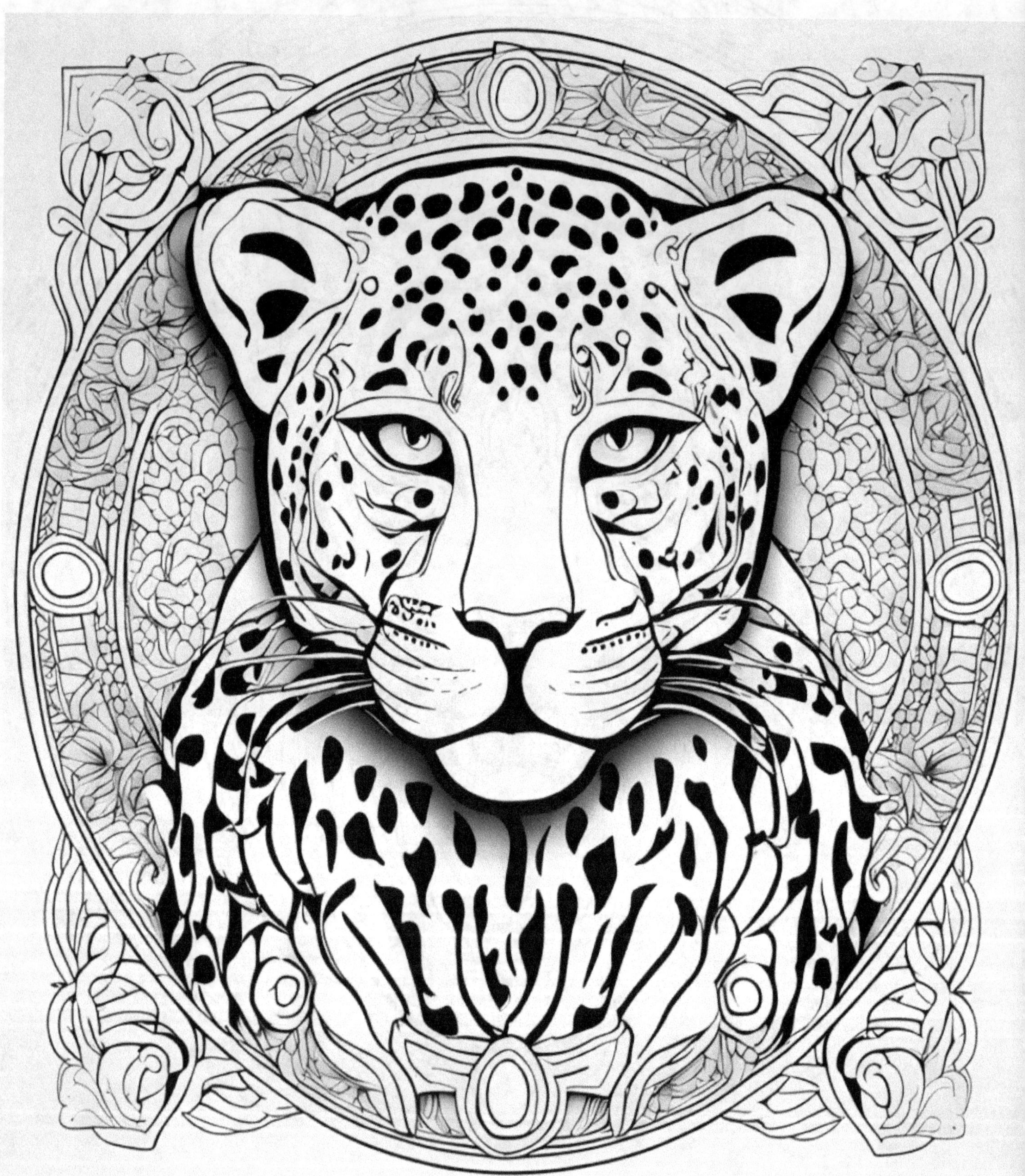

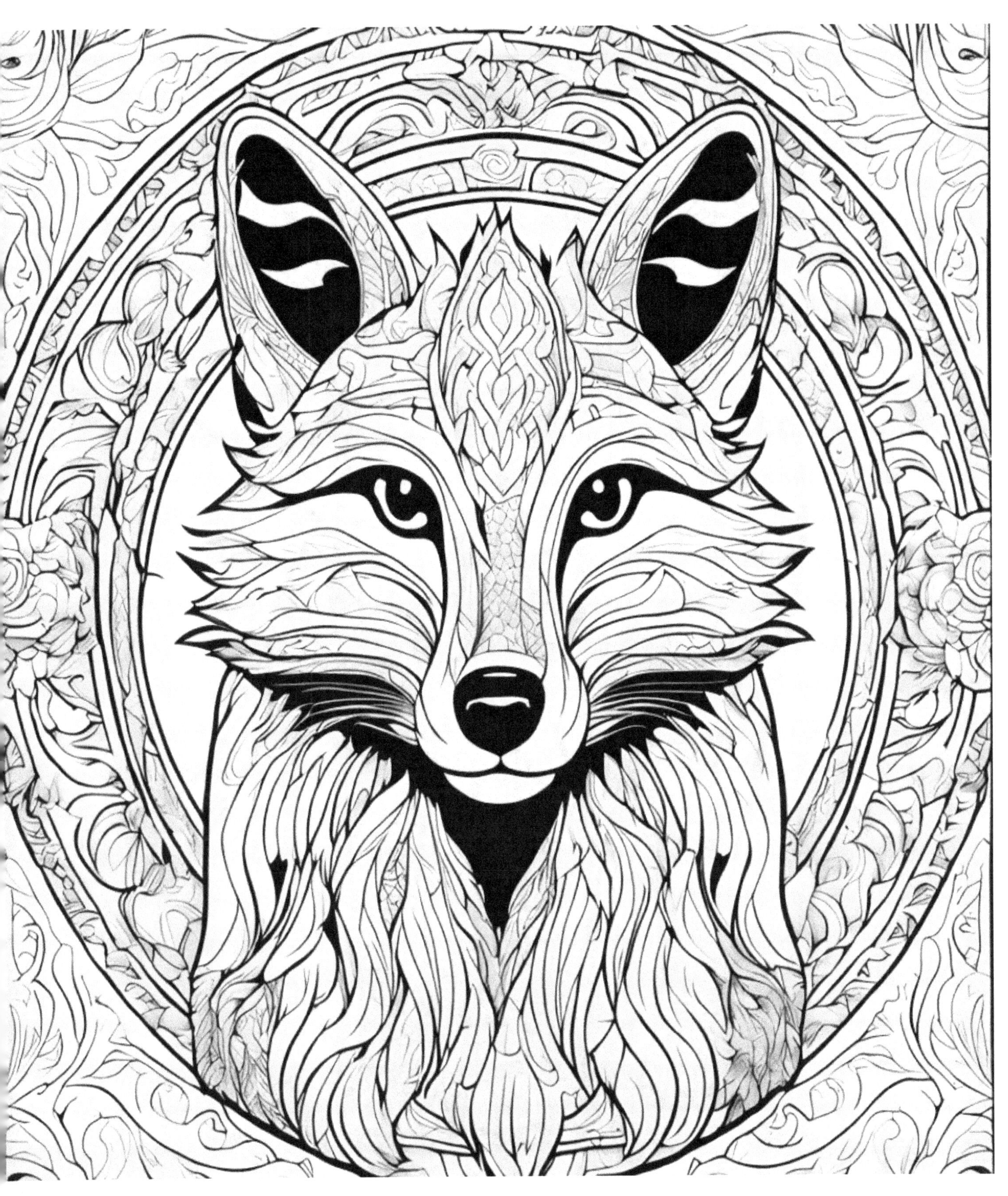

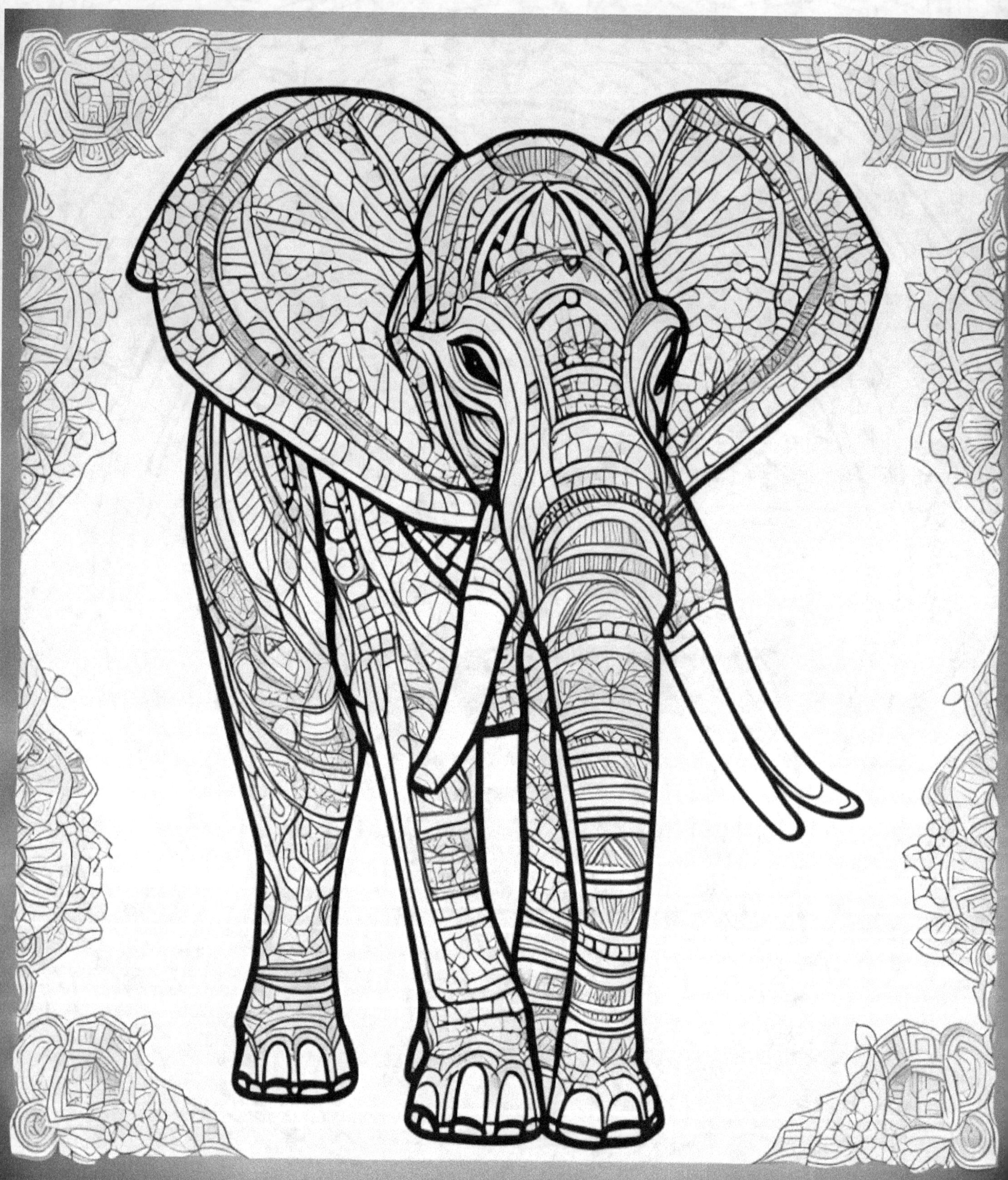

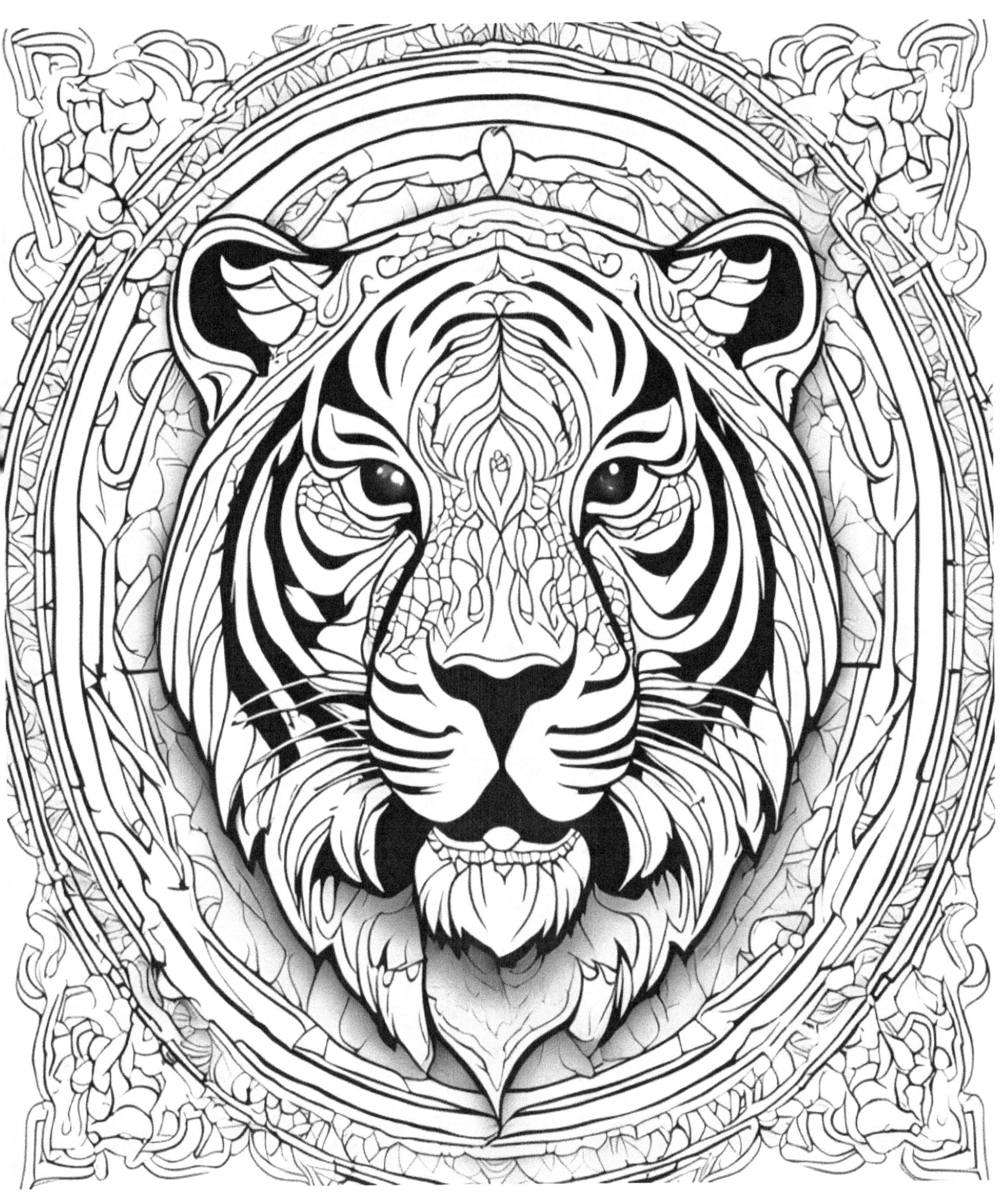

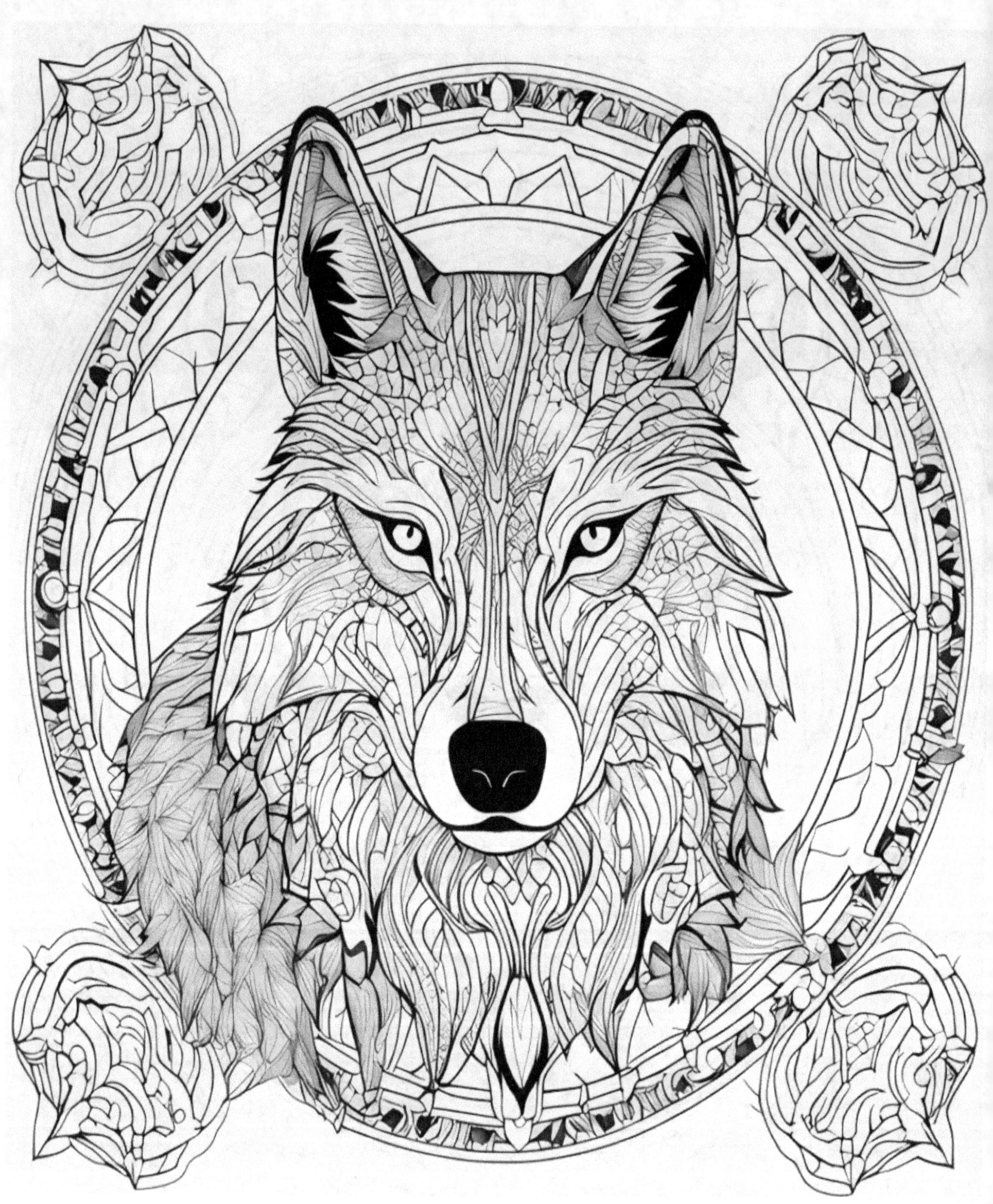

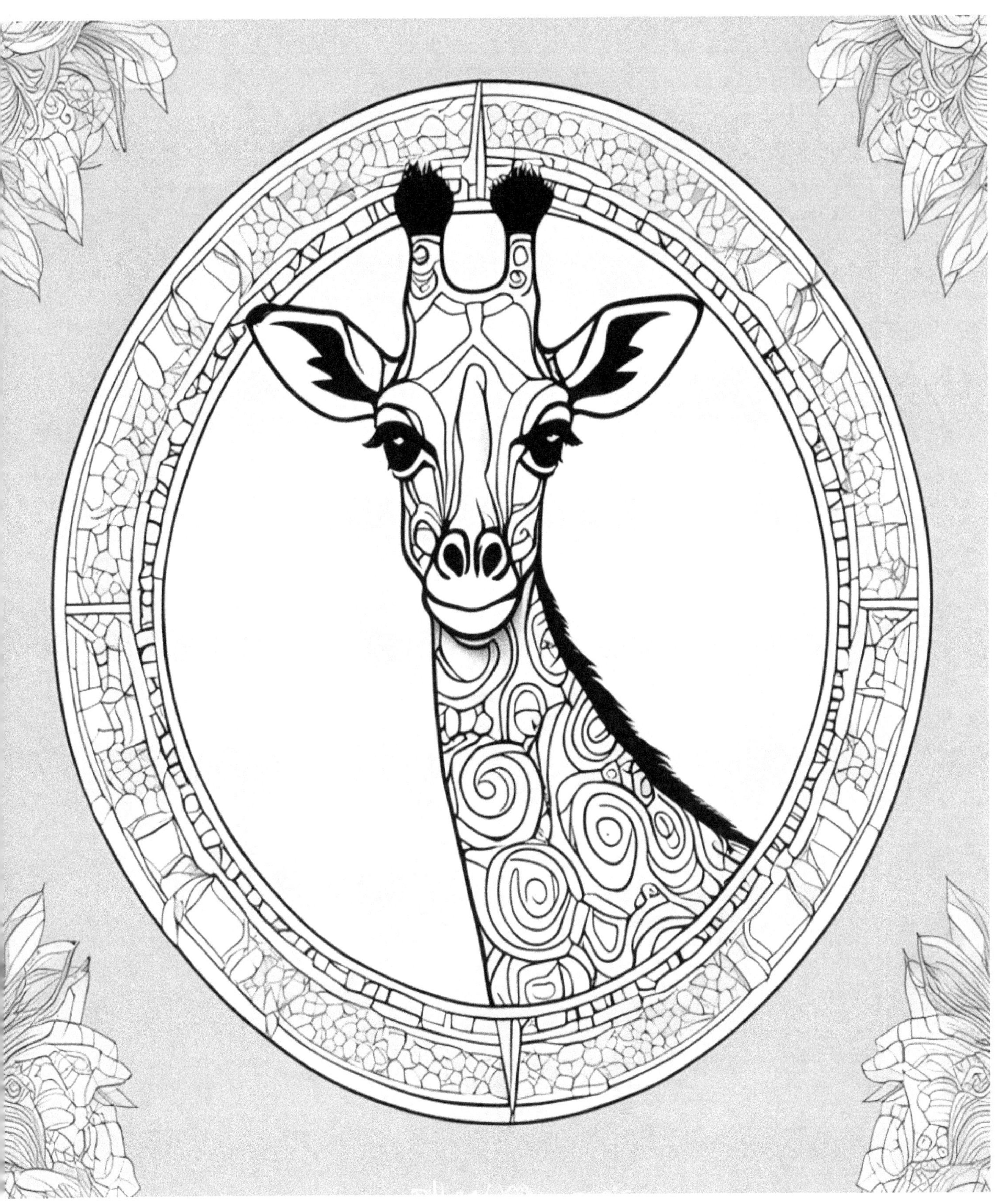

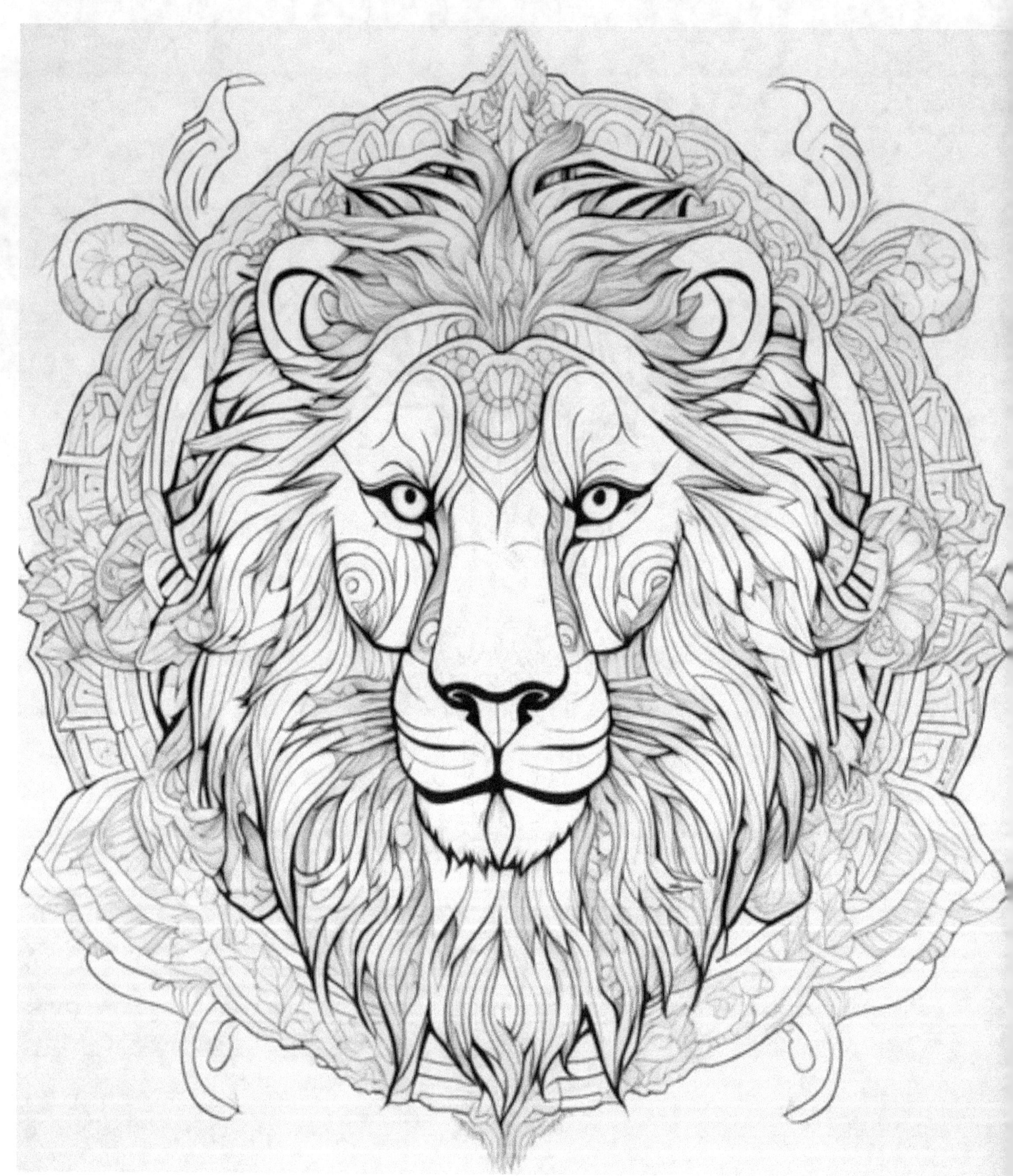

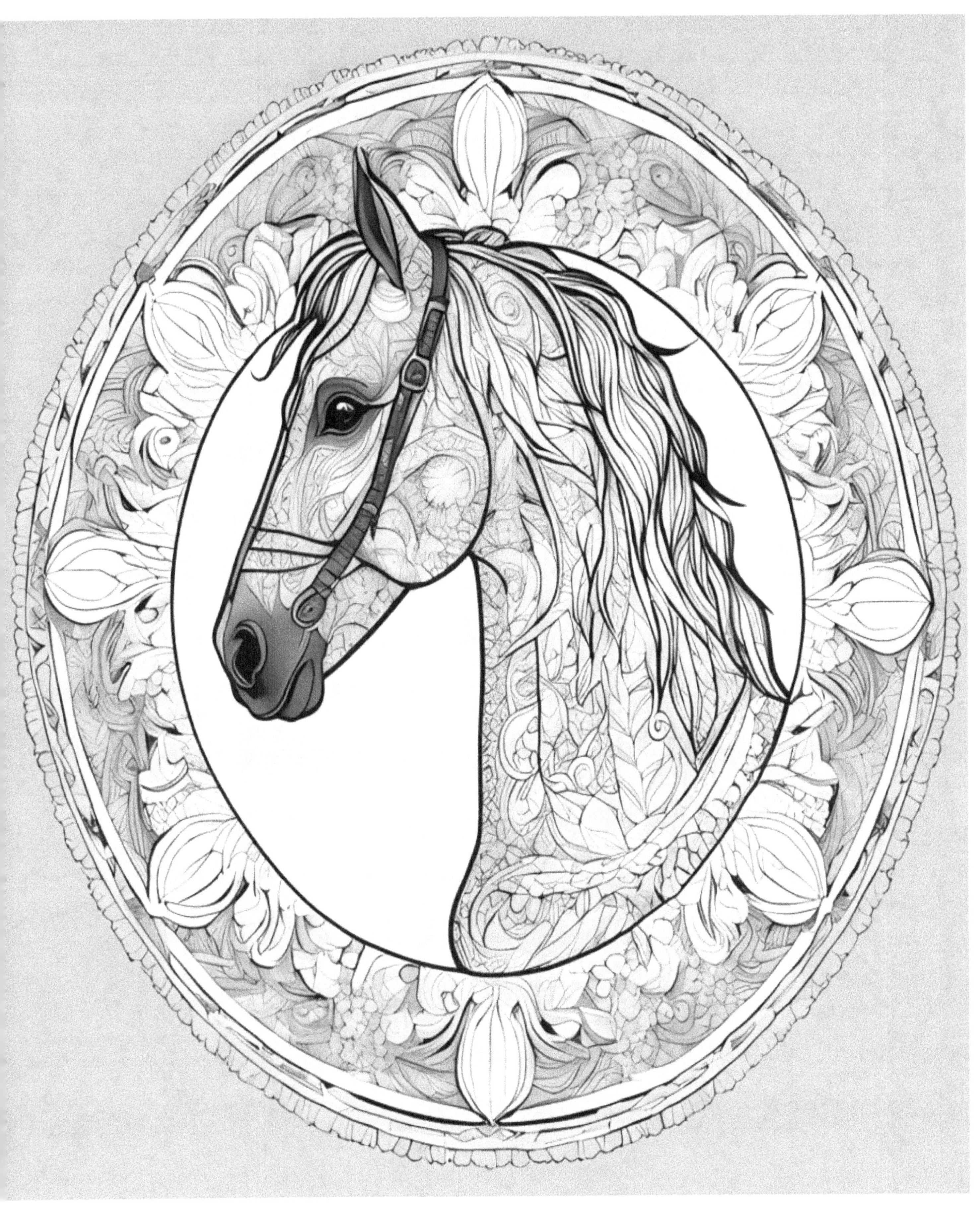

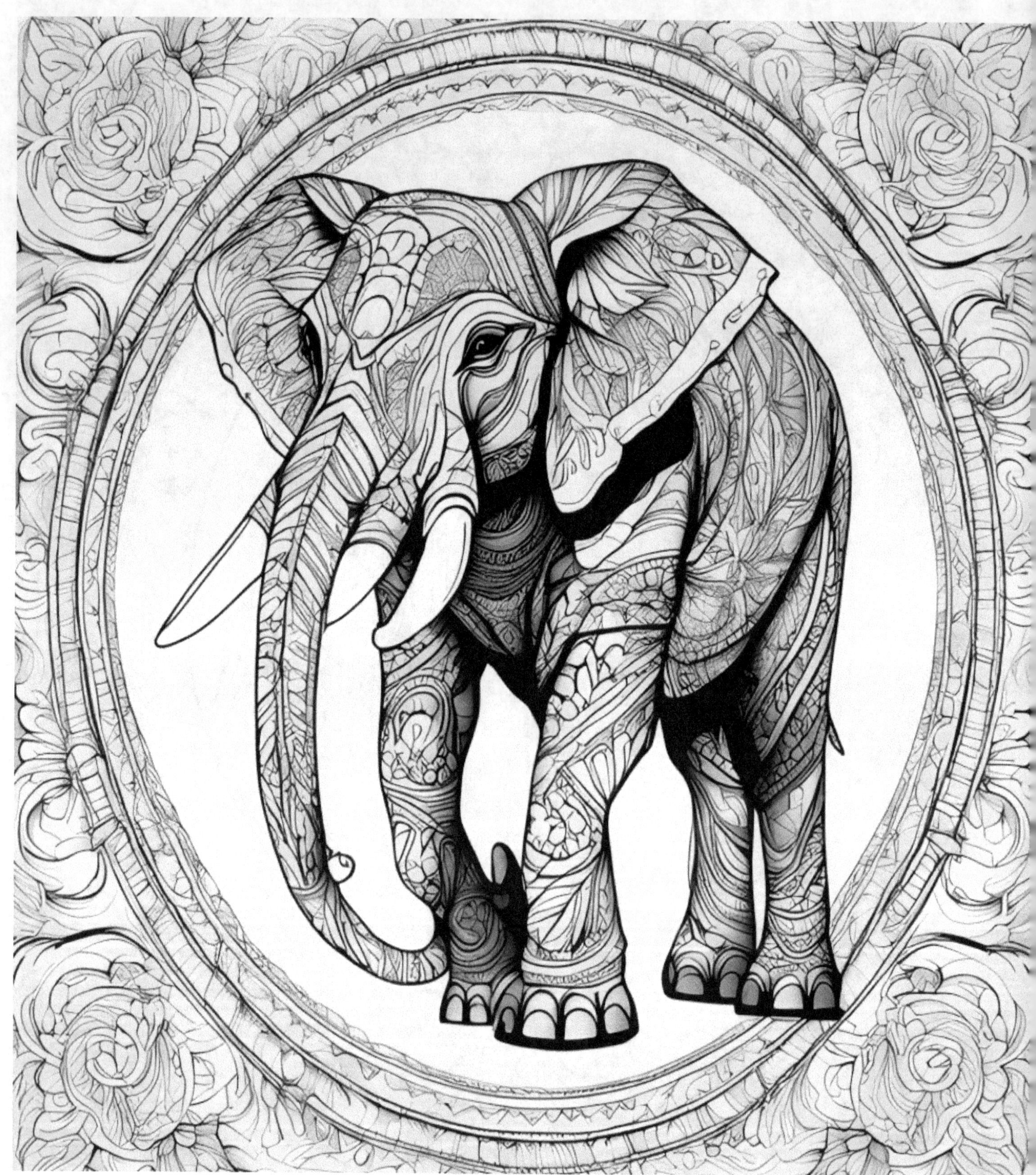

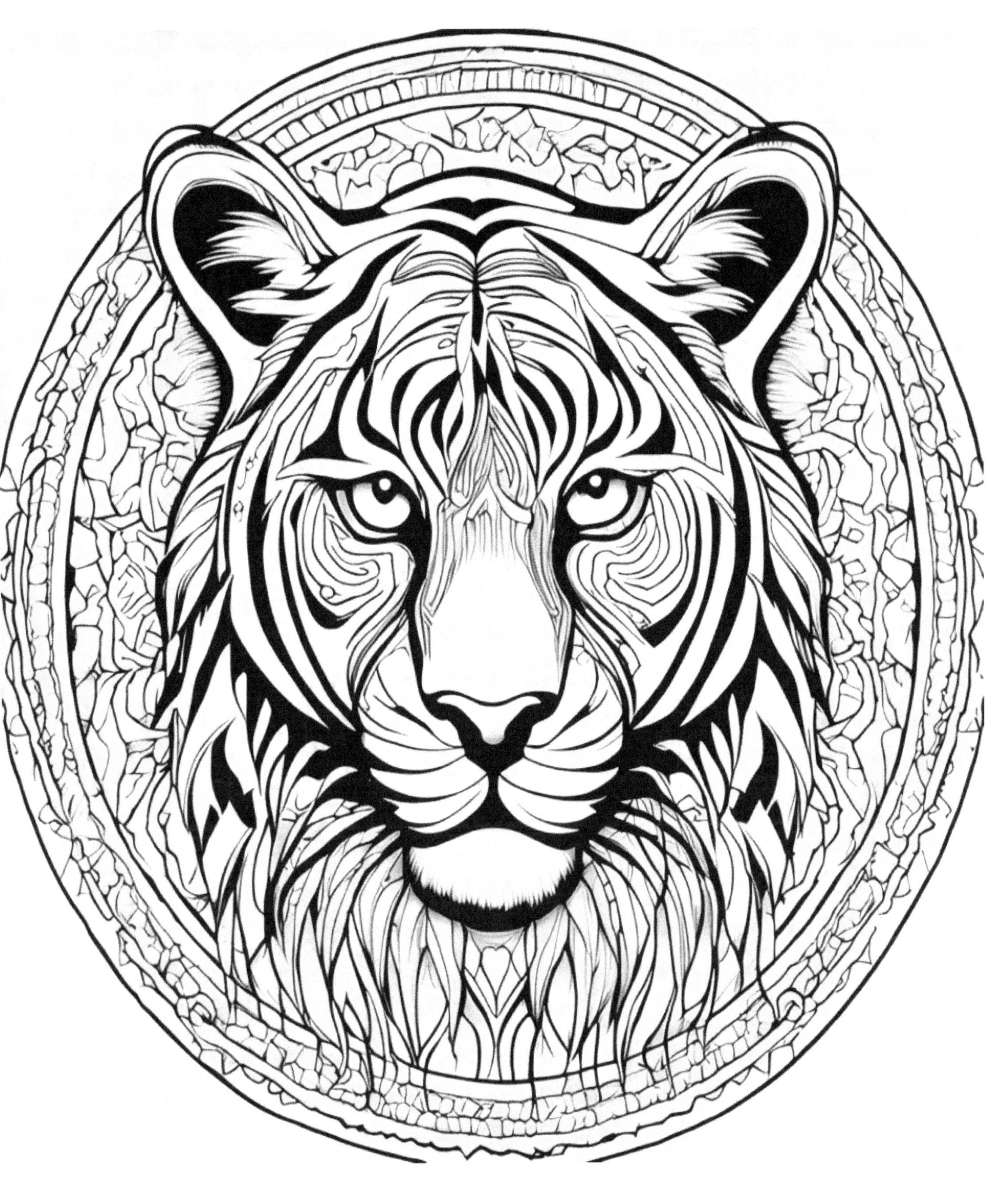

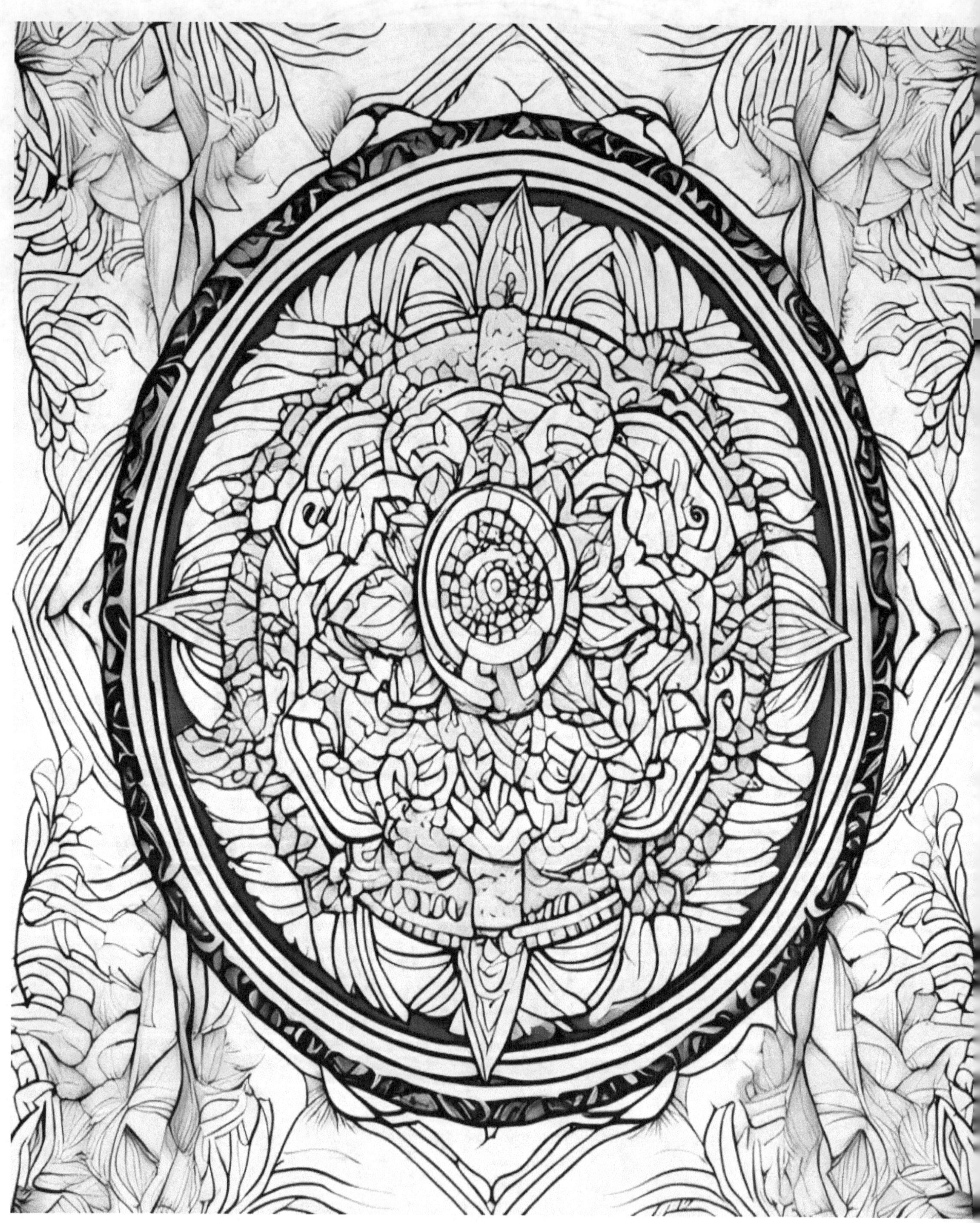